What Our Readers Have Said...

"Although I consider myself a seasoned sales professional, it is helpful to have past learning's refreshed. The books were also beneficial because of the information concerning 'trends' in the sales relationship. The sales process should be viewed as dynamic since business relationships change regularly."

•

"For the particular business I am in and the type of sales calls I have, I find that the books in the Pinpoint Sales Training Series are very often applicable to how I conduct business. I would recommend them to other sales people, just not ones that are in my industry."

•

"These books provide very good concepts. It fits in well with the Bell Leadership training program that I attended in November."

•

"I use this material in these books and apply it to my customers and other employees I work with."

•

"I would like to know other topics. Is there anything on Production Management or Consultative Selling or Time Management?"

•

"These books are great tools that should be used as guidelines for our everyday

supervisory practices. You need to take the time to do a short self-evaluation when reading them."

•

"The Pinpoint Training Series delivers information that could be used in a lot different areas."

•

"I like this because I can take them with me to read at a convenient time. I feel the little time I have to spend in the office is best use on activities that directly relate to revenue opportunities. I like the short amount of time it takes to keep up with these."

•

"I prefer the self-study approach; it fits in with my schedule."

•

"My thought is that the real value of these books comes into effect when doing the action plans."

•

"Short and sweet. These books are easy to comprehend."

•

"I have enjoyed reading these books. They are relevant to today's work environment and the ongoing change in the way we manage our workforce."

•

"I do feel that these books have been very helpful to me at my job."

•

"I think a lot of the recommendations in these books are very useful, and can be applicable to everyday situations. If nothing else, it's a good reference guide to fall back upon if a situation arises in the future."

•

"These books are relevant to today's work environment and the ongoing change in the way we manage our workforce."

•

Cold Calling

Pinpoint Sales Skill Development Training Series

TIMOTHY F. BEDNARZ

MAJORIUM
BUSINESS PRESS

Pinpoint Sales Skill Development Training Series
"Cold Calling"
Timothy F. Bednarz

Graphic design: Monika Pawlak

Majorium Business Press
2025 Main Street
Stevens Point, WI 54481
715.342.1018 • 800.654.4935

ISBN 978-1-882181-45-2

Printed in the United States of America

Introduction

The Pinpoint Sales Skill Development Training Series is designed for targeted training and education regarding increased improvement in a specific skill or competency.

Each book within this series is designed to be easy to use, understand and apply to your job. It can be used as a basis for training individuals, as a discussion guide or as a personal training tool.

Each chapter within this book discusses a specific concept. When you have completed all eight chapters you should have a 360° perspective of the topic.

Additionally, each chapter is divided into specific sections:

- The first section provides you with an overview of the topic
- The Implications section discusses why the concept is important, and why it is important to learn and apply.
- The Strategies, Tips & Techniques to Apply section teaches how to use and apply the particular concept to your work.
- The Points to Ponder section gives you something to think about or to be discussed with a group setting. These are questions not meant to be immediately answered, but to be pondered over time.
- The Training Activity section provides you with the tools to transfer what you have learned to your job. It is designed to help create an action plan to effectively apply the concept.

Each of the topics in this series is time-tested and proven in the marketplace. They have been used by thousands of employees as training tools. Many of the users have commented that what made these books valuable, was the ability to refer to them when a problem surfaced. They indicated that they remembered reading about the exact problem. They referred back to these books and found an appropriate solution.

You will find them equally valuable as a resource in your professional development library.

Table of Contents

1. Easing Your Way into Cold Calling 1

2. Handling Call Reluctance 5

3. Why Twenty Percent Succeed? 9

4. Developing a Cold Calling Strategy 13

5. The Role of Persistence in Cold Calling 17

6. Reaching the Decision Maker 21

7. Getting Past the Gatekeeper 25

8. The First Thirty Seconds 29

LEARNING OBJECTIVES:

- To understand the importance of cold calling.
- To establish cold calling goals and objectives.
- To determine the best cold calling method.
- To set up an effective cold calling system.
- To develop techniques to get past a gatekeeper.
- To apply strategies to get the decision maker's attention.

1

Easing Your Way into Cold Calling

Many salespeople are opposed to the prospect of cold calling and the rejection that comes with it. Yet, cold calling is an essential skill in gaining and retaining customers.

Every successful salesman or woman builds his or her business on cold calling. They realize that the pipeline must be kept full if new and exciting sales opportunities are to present themselves.

IMPLICATIONS – WHAT THIS MEANS TO YOU

The biggest stumbling block for most salespeople is the fear of rejection when they cold call. However, successful salespeople are aware of the numbers game, and realize that every "no" brings them that much closer to a "yes." When they encounter rejection, they simply move on to the next prospect.

Salespeople must clearly understand and comprehend that rejection is a business decision. When a prospect says "no" what is really being said is: "I'm not interested or I have no need." The rejection is not and should not be taken personally—most prospects don't know a cold calling salesperson well enough to make a personal judgment—yet many people do react this way and get discouraged. Consequently, they are not as effective as they could be when cold calling.

STRATEGIES, TIPS & TECHNIQUES TO APPLY

There are a few techniques that can be used to make cold calling more effective with less negative consequences.

Use Voicemail

The reality of cold calling is that no matter how hard salespeople try to reach them, they will rarely get the prospect without numerous attempts. They can quickly make 40 or 50 calls in an afternoon and most often will get a secretary—who will then give them voicemail.

Many salespeople hesitate to leave a voicemail message when cold calling. In the current environment, however, if salespeople want to be successful, they must leave a message according to the following guidelines:

- Leave a concise message of no more than 20 seconds clearly stating two or three benefits of using your product or service.
- Keep a readily available file listing who was called on and the reason(s) for calling.
- Have a prepared response ready for when the call is returned. First impressions count: if salespeople fumble and stumble through a response they will significantly diminish their chances of getting the prospect interested.
- Rehearse callback responses until they are smooth and natural.

Send Introductions

An introduction letter, fax or email makes your call less intrusive. It's the repeated contact that leads to the sale. The more a prospect becomes familiar with a salesperson's name, the more likely they will be to open the door to a sale.

If salespeople promise to call on a certain date at a certain time, it should be kept, as the more punctual they are, the more successful they will be. (Care should be taken not to overdo it, as salespeople can be perceived as a pest with too many contacts.)

Don't Procrastinate

Many salespeople will use call preparation as an excuse to procrastinate or avoid making calls. They will fumble through folders and sales books to collect information and organize themselves. Time, calls and work should be planned the night before, and the sales day devoted to selling on the phone or in person.

Develop a System

A cold calling system—whether a simple legal pad or expensive system produced by Day Timer or Time Design—should include the company, contact, phone number and reason for calling. As one call is completed, it should be checked off, with the list worked until every name has been contacted. A systematized approach will increase productivity and decrease procrastination.

Be Aware of the Prospect's Environment

As the typical manager is interrupted by phone, email, fax and mail over 200 times per day, their time and space must be respected. Salespeople should be careful to ask whether "this is a good time" to talk with them. If not, a phone appointment at a more convenient time should be requested. The salesperson's emphasis must be to show that he or she is there to suggest ways the customer can improve their business.

Focus on the Purpose

It is unrealistic to expect to make a sale on the first cold call. Cold calling is a process of planting seeds in prospect's minds, as it generally takes up to eight calls before they are sold.

Salespeople should use cold calling to gather information by qualifying the customer and gaining an appointment. They should not try to sell at this point of the process, but, avoiding gimmicks to gain attention, they should get to the point, state their business, and quickly demonstrate their value to the prospect.

POINTS TO PONDER — SOMETHING TO THINK ABOUT

1. How organized are you in your efforts to get the information you need quickly and effectively when cold calling?
2. Do you use introductory letters, emails or faxes before you cold call? Do they increase your ability to make contact with the prospect rather than voicemail?

TRAINING ACTIVITY — APPLICATION & ACTION PLAN

1. Average the time it takes to convert a cold call into an actual face-to-face meeting.
2. Compare averages and results with other salespeople. Create a list from their input that may offer new and fresh ideas to add to your collection of cold calling techniques.
3. Star the ones that seem to work more effectively.
4. Address organizational skills that work well to remain on top of your prospects.

2

Handling Call Reluctance

Many salespeople fear the rejection that comes with making cold calls and are reluctant to make the necessary efforts to fill their pipeline. However, the most successful salespeople have literally no call reluctance, and actually relish making cold calls. Well-versed in the mathematics of selling, they understand that every rejection is one step closer to a sale. They have spent the time to analyze their call patterns, and know that for every 10 or 20 phone calls they will get an appointment. Out of every 5 to 10 appointments, they will get a sale. While the formula will vary among salespeople, there is a definite statistical pattern for success.

IMPLICATIONS — WHAT THIS MEANS TO YOU

Many salespeople experience some fear of failure and rejection that translates into some form of call reluctance. It isn't easy to deal with rejection on a daily and consistent basis—a unique aspect of the sales profession. The ability to understand and handle rejection is what separates the successful salesperson from others.

This is important to salespeople because unless they understand the vast majority of the rejection they experience is not a personal judgment about their abilities or them as a person, but a simple business decision regarding the product they are selling, they will never be able to overcome the associated fear. Quite simply, not every company has a need or use for the products a salesperson has to sell. However, many do, and a salesperson will not discover which ones until he or she makes the initial contact. Many opportunities will reveal themselves if the fear of contact is eliminated or at least placed on the back burner.

If salespeople further understand the mathematics of their call patterns, then rejection is easier to accept. They automatically know that every rejection brings them a step closer to a sale.

STRATEGIES, TIPS & TECHNIQUES TO APPLY

Before salespeople are able to overcome and handle their personal call reluctance, they must understand the underlying reasons behind it, bring their fears to the surface, and take action to overcome them.

Some strategies to overcome a salesperson's call reluctance include:

Examine the Causes of Sales Fears

Most individuals exaggerate their personal anxieties. In reality, the consequences are far less serious than what they actually feared in the first place. Salespeople must examine the underlying causes of their fears by determining the things that can actually happen when they make a cold call. An examination of all of the possible reactions to a salesperson's cold call reveals the following:

- The prospect can hang up on the salesperson.
- The prospect can be rude.
- The salesperson will reach the prospect's voicemail.
- The prospect will listen to what the salesperson actually has to say.
- The prospect will be glad the salesperson called.

The worst two consequences of a cold call are that a prospect will be rude and hang up on the salesperson. These are two easily accepted consequences that most salespeople can readily handle without difficulty.

Focus on a Purpose

One of the primary pitfalls many salespeople stumble into when they make cold calls is that they actually attempt to make a sale. Since securing a sale is unlikely, salespeople should limit their overall focus on getting an appointment with the prospect. This reduces the risk to the prospect and allows the salesperson to build a solid foundation upon which to establish a future sale. Salespeople should worry about the sale after they get in front of the prospect.

Have a Goal

Consistency builds sales. For a salesperson to keep his or her pipeline filled with viable prospects, they need to create a minimum and consistent call level. This means execution of a cold calling strategy such as making at least one appointment a day or conducting four or five follow-ups. To achieve success, salespeople must have the personal discipline to execute this strategy daily.

Track the Results

Sales metrics can be a beneficial and motivational tool for every salesperson to use. An effective sales pipeline will include a high number of cold calls resulting in a diminishing number of appointments, presentations, and product trials and ultimately sales. There is a direct correlation between each level of the sale.

Salespeople should track the number of cold calls they need to make before they are able to get one appointment. Then they need to track the number of appointments needed to get a sale. Successful salespeople monitor and record the running average of these statistics and use these numbers to manage their sales activities and increase their overall performance.

POINTS TO PONDER — SOMETHING TO THINK ABOUT

1. What do you fear will happen to you when you make a cold call?
2. What do you focus on when you make a call?
3. Have you established a daily goal for appointments and follow-up calls? Do you follow it consistently? Why or why not?

TRAINING ACTIVITY — APPLICATION & ACTION PLAN

1. Track the number of cold calls you need to make before you are able to get an appointment.
2. Then track the number of appointments you need to obtain before you actually gain a sale.
3. Keep a running average of these statistics.

3

Why Twenty Percent Succeed?

The worst situation for a salesperson to be in is to have run out of viable prospects to call on. The best way to assure that this does not happen is to cold call—the best way to acquire and meet new business prospects.

Despite many trends to the contrary, there is only one main way to get new business. This is not marketing and advertising, but knocking on doors or using the telephone to get an appointment.

IMPLICATIONS – WHAT THIS MEANS TO YOU

Salespeople who consistently make cold calls will excel. Cold calling is an excellent way for salespeople to experiment in order to develop and strengthen their skills. The additional—and primary—benefit is that it represents a proven way of acquiring and developing new customers.

Cold calling is an essential skill for salespeople to possess if they wish to become successful in their field. Not only does cold calling keep their pipeline filled with prospects and improve their selling skills, but it also provides them with an important source of customer and competitive information that they otherwise would not have.

STRATEGIES, TIPS & TECHNIQUES TO APPLY

A sale cannot be made until the salesperson identifies and targets a prospect. Many salespeople are comfortable in their territories, highlighting and skimming the most profitable business or calling on existing customers. In fact, 80% of salespeople fail to explore their territories' full potential. The other 20% are always looking for new sources of business.

The factors that differentiate the two groups and separate the truly successful salespeople from the average ones include:

An Understanding of the Mechanics of Selling

Successful salespeople understand the mechanics of selling through an easy application of mathematics. The specific numbers will vary by individual salespeople, their product and industry, but the formula will remain the same. It takes x number of cold calls to get an appointment. It takes x number of appointments to make a presentation or product trial, and it takes x presentations or trials to get the sale. To fill in these numbers, salespeople must begin to track their activities. Once they benchmark their activities, if they wish to increase their sales, they must add one or two cold calls per day. It's that simple.

Consistency

Understanding the basic mechanics of selling, successful salespeople consistently make cold calling a part of their daily activities. They develop a targeted number of cold calls they need to make every day to keep the pipeline filled with qualified prospects. This is a dedicated discipline they never stray from.

Persistence

Cold calling can be frustrating due to the high degree of failure and rejection associated with it. Successful salespeople understand the need to persist in the face of failure. They know that while the average salesperson quits calling after one or two calls, the sale is often made after the eighth or ninth call.

No Call Reluctance

Successful salespeople have no call reluctance. Well-versed in the mechanics of selling, they know that every rejection brings them one step closer to the next sale. Rather than getting frustrated, their motivation remains unchanged when a prospect rejects them.

No Fear of Rejection

Successful salespeople understand the majority of cold calls made result in rejection. They know and expect it, and don't fear it. They take it in stride and make sure they celebrate their successes to keep themselves motivated and confident in their abilities.

No Fear of Failure

Selling is a profession built upon a series of failures. Successful salespeople know they are going to fail—in fact, more often than they will succeed—but they understand that each failure allows them to learn more, improve their skills and ultimately become emotionally stronger. With time and experience, they are able to shrug off failure as part of their jobs.

Business development is a primary responsibility of salespeople and it cannot be accomplished without strong cold calling skills. Rather than being sensitive to failure and rejection, salespeople must understand that these are not personal judgments of their ability or skill level, but business decisions. This is the critical barrier most must overcome if they wish to excel in their profession.

POINTS TO PONDER — SOMETHING TO THINK ABOUT

1. Do you embrace or resist cold calling? Why?
2. What has been your success with cold calling? Does it meet your expectations?

TRAINING ACTIVITY — APPLICATION & ACTION PLAN

1. Benchmark your sales activities over the next 30 days in order to determine:
   - How many cold calls you need to make to gain an appointment.
   - How many appointments you need to make a formal presentation or product demonstration.
   - How many sales presentations or product demonstrations are needed to make a sale.
2. If there are other critical steps in your individual sales process, track those also.

4

Developing a Cold Calling Strategy

In the past salespeople could go door-to-door or make endless calls with a high degree of probability of meeting or talking with a prospective customer. Times have changed. Managers and buyers don't have the time to see an unscheduled salesperson and many will not even agree to an appointment unless the salesperson has clearly demonstrated their value beforehand. They don't have the time or patience to educate a salesperson about their business.

Salespeople must have an established cold calling strategy to maximize their time and to produce results that make the effort worthwhile.

IMPLICATIONS – WHAT THIS MEANS TO YOU

Cold calling is becoming increasingly difficult for several reasons. Waves of layoffs and downsizing have eliminated many levels of management in most companies. This results in fewer people handling more responsibility. The rapid increases in technology have made the same people more efficient, making their increased responsibilities possible. However, it also has contributed the second barrier to cold calling—the electronic veil.

More individuals have entrenched themselves behind an electronic veil of voice and email to screen and filter out the overwhelming number of messages they receive every business day.

Salespeople must use persistence and creativity to pierce the electronic veil in any way possible. Persistence alone is not sufficient to pierce the electronic veil.

STRATEGIES, TIPS & TECHNIQUES TO APPLY

Salespeople must have a predetermined cold calling strategy that encompasses and employs their experience, expertise and creativity. A singular, "one size fits all" approach is ineffective. Rather, salespeople are better served to develop prospects in small-targeted groups that allow them to glean specific information before they make the first call. Doing this includes:

Research and Preparation

Salespeople must take the time to learn about the prospect before they make the first call. In essence they are pre-qualifying the prospect to determine if they are a worthwhile investment of time and effort.

This can be done through several means beginning with an examination of the prospect's website, sales materials or other sources of factual information. Additional facts can be gleaned from an informational call either in person or by telephone. During this call, the salesperson will talk with receptionists and/or assistants to identify decision makers, products, etc.

The Initial Call Strategy

Salespeople typically have less than 30 seconds to spark a prospect's interest. This is why preparation is important. When salespeople have thoroughly prepared themselves, they can develop one or two key benefits that might interest a prospect sufficiently to expand the conversation. The first 30-second hurdle is one of the biggest obstacles salespeople have to overcome. Once they have sparked a prospect's interest, more time will be allotted to discuss the customer's needs in greater detail by effectively probing to confirm the information uncovered by research and preparation.

One of the pitfalls salespeople easily stumble into when cold calling is attempting to make the sale during the first call. This is not likely to happen. The primary purpose of the initial call is to determine the customer's interest and to sell the customer on the need to schedule an appointment.

How to Cold Call

Many salespeople wonder what the best strategy is to cold call. The answer varies. Salespeople must use their creativity and expertise to pierce the electronic veil.

Voicemail

Conventional wisdom states that a salesperson should never leave a voicemail message. In reality, unless the salesperson leaves a message, it is unlikely that they will ever talk to a potential customer. The best solution is to leave a variation of the initial 30-second introduction to "tease" the customer. Leaving a message solely regarding your name and company is unlikely to elicit a response. A highly creative voicemail can sufficiently spark a customer's interest to call back.

Email

Busy executives who refuse to return phone calls often will respond to an email. A business solicitation is not spam. The key is to keep the initial email message short and to the point. As a customer responds, the length and depth of the email discussion can expand. Once again a variation of the initial 30-second introduction is appropriate.

Other Creative Methods

There are a host of other methods and techniques that salespeople can use to get the prospective customer's attention. Salespeople have used gimmicks such as singing telegrams, newspaper articles of interest and unique gifts. It is up to the creative imagination of the individual salesperson to develop an idea that gets him or her recognized. The key is to think outside of the box and create an idea that is both clever and unique.

POINTS TO PONDER — SOMETHING TO THINK ABOUT

1. Explain how you cold call. What is your most effective strategy?
2. How successful are your cold calling efforts?

TRAINING ACTIVITY — APPLICATION & ACTION PLAN

Develop an idea or concept that you can use to get your point across while getting the customer's attention.

1. After targeting a specific customer, develop a single concept of what you wish to communicate.
2. What kind of prop or tool can you use to communicate your idea?
3. How will you deliver the idea and information to the customer?

5

The Role of Persistence in Cold Calling

It is amazing how many salespeople will make one or two cold calls on a prospect and move on to what they perceive as more likely customers. What is even more amazing is that the same salespeople are surrendering valuable sales to their competition without a whimper.

The natural conclusion most salespeople arrive at when they cold call is that the prospect is "not interested." Not interested does not mean there is no need or that the prospect couldn't benefit from the salesperson's product or service. In most cases, the harried potential buyer is too busy or focused on other matters to talk with salespeople. Many salespeople take this response at face value and move on to other prospects.

IMPLICATIONS — WHAT THIS MEANS TO YOU

If a prospect has a need for a product and can afford its purchase, then it is the responsibility of the salesperson to sell him or her. Yet, many salespeople never allow themselves to determine if the prospect falls into this category since they have accepted a brush-off from the prospect.

Good salespeople understand that many worthwhile sales must be earned. This means being persistent until the prospect is willing to allow the sales process to move forward. Many salespeople will skim their territories for the easy sale, but the real gems must be worked for, and this means persisting until the sale is made.

STRATEGIES, TIPS & TECHNIQUES TO APPLY

There are many excellent reasons why salespeople must be persistent in their cold calling. These include:

Things Change

The main reason that salespeople must persist in their cold calling efforts is that things change. Buyers switch jobs and positions, and circumstances change quickly. Technology, the economy and world events have a massive impact on the rates of change most companies experience. Without becoming a nuisance, salespeople need to cold call on prospects on a regular and ongoing basis.

Additionally, many sales are not made due to poor timing. At the time of an initial cold call, the prospect may not have a need, while several months later the timing and circumstances may have altered sufficiently for the sale to move forward. Still many salespeople maintain the initial perception that the prospect does not have a need based upon their first response.

As circumstances change, many opportunities arise. Contrary to most opinions, surveys show that most companies do not necessarily use their existing supplier when a new opportunity arises. Typically, the salesperson that is there at the right time is the one who gets the sale, which is only possible when they cold call on a regular basis.

Slowly Builds Trust and Rapport

As salespeople are consistent in their contacts with prospects, trust and rapport are slowly built and developed. These are critical elements that salespeople must establish before a sale can be made. While the prospect may not provide a lot of time at any given point, a relationship will slowly develop.

Additionally, many salespeople often make one call and move on to other prospects. When salespeople regularly call, prospects develop the perception that the salesperson is not looking for a quick sale, but is indeed interested in earning their business.

Builds Awareness and Credibility

Salespeople want to develop customer awareness so that when an opportunity does arise, their name and company will come to mind. When a problem occurs, prospects seek quick solutions. When they are familiar with a salesperson, they will most likely contact him or her to inquire about a solution.

No potential customer recalls a single cold call. However, the salesperson who calls regularly will be remembered and recalled when the opportunity arises.

Overcomes Sales Resistance

In many cases, persistent and regular cold calling will overcome initial sales resistance. Many prospects may be inclined to give salespeople a chance at their business after they have called long enough. Persistence has built the necessary trust and rapport to provide the salesperson a portion of their business. Often a good salesperson sees this opportunity as the chance they have been waiting for to demonstrate his or her value to the prospect.

Being Tested By the Prospect

It is not uncommon for prospects to test salespeople who call upon them. Many are aware that there are numerous salespeople eager for a quick sale, who will quickly disappear once it is made. Prospects want salespeople to earn their business and respect their value as a potential customer. Therefore, many will gauge how persistent a salesperson is before they give them a chance to develop their business.

POINTS TO PONDER — SOMETHING TO THINK ABOUT

1. How many calls do you make before you stop calling on a prospect?
2. Can you cite an example that demonstrates how persistence has resulted in a sale?

TRAINING ACTIVITY — APPLICATION & ACTION PLAN

Develop a long-term cold calling strategy for resistant or hard-to-contact prospects.

1. Determine a regular calling schedule.
2. Identify a cold calling strategy detailing specific objectives for each call.
3. Create mail, fax and email follow-ups that you can use for each call.

6

Reaching the Decision Maker

Reaching a decision maker during cold calling can be a daunting task. Many are too busy and focused on their responsibilities to be disrupted by salespeople calling to pitch their products and services.

Salespeople must establish a method that gets the decision maker's attention and allows a salesperson to demonstrate the value he or she provides through their product or service.

IMPLICATIONS – WHAT THIS MEANS TO YOU

Prospects are barraged with countless sales messages every day. These are not limited to salespeople's calls on them, and include radio, television, direct mail and pop-up ads on the Internet. This adds to the increasing amounts of clutter of sales messages that salespeople must rise above in order to be heard.

Salespeople are not selling in a void, they are competing for the prospect's time and attention. Traditional selling methods are minimized. Salespeople must look at more creative means to get their message communicated, leveraging the available technologies to maximize impact.

STRATEGIES, TIPS & TECHNIQUES TO APPLY

It comes as no surprise that the majority of prospects are entrenched behind an electronic veil that seems difficult, if not impossible, to penetrate. However, there are strategies that greatly enhance the salesperson's ability to get the decision maker's attention and ultimately be able to contact them face-to-face.

Since the majority of cold calling occurs over the telephone, the following technique will focus on maximizing the salesperson's effectiveness on it.

The first step is to create a set of sales pieces that can be faxed and emailed. A faxed sales piece should be clean and uncluttered with generous white space for easy readability. It should be no longer than one to two pages, ideally one page.

An email piece offers more flexibility. A four-color sales piece can be created and developed into a PDF file that is easily attached to any email. Additionally, a one-page sales piece can be saved as a GIF or JPG file and attached to the email. When the intended individual opens his or her email, the sales piece will be displayed in the text box.

The initial sales piece needs to highlight several key benefits to spark the prospect's interest. It should be attractive and concise in the information it transmits. Salespeople should stay away from any hype or gimmicks in these presentations.

Once a salesperson has prepared these two pieces, he or she can begin to make cold calls. When a call is placed, the salesperson should inquire and obtain the name of the appropriate decision maker. The name, title and responsibilities should be confirmed. A fax number or email address should also be requested. If the receptionist does not have this information or is not allowed to disclose it, the salesperson should request to speak with the decision maker's assistant or secretary. When the salesperson is connected to this individual, the same information should be requested again. It is likely the decision maker's assistant will comply with these requests. Salespeople should not forget to inquire as to what is the best time to contact the decision maker.

Salespeople should make sure they are friendly with the receptionist and the decision maker's assistant. These people can become allies and help them get through to the decision maker.

Once the salesperson gathers this necessary information, they should immediately send a fax or email with an introductory note to the decision maker.

The salesperson should make a follow-up call to the decision maker within 24 hours. If he or she was polite and friendly, it is likely the receptionist or decision maker's assistant will help him or her in every way. Additionally, the decision maker already has received the essential information and will expect the salesperson's follow-up.

POINTS TO PONDER — SOMETHING TO THINK ABOUT

1. What methods have you effectively used to reach a decision maker?
2. Can you think of any other methods to reach decision makers effectively?

TRAINING ACTIVITY — APPLICATION & ACTION PLAN

Develop an effective cold calling sales piece.

1. Identify three essential benefits that should spark the decision maker's interest.
2. Develop a sales piece around these benefits. Use bulleted lists for easy readability.
3. Include a customer's testimonial that demonstrates the benefits to the prospect.
4. Include all of your contact information.
5. Design a clean looking and concise fax. Use plenty of white space and keep it to a single page.

6. Design an attractive sales piece that can be developed into a PDF file using the same information. If you need assistance, contract a graphic artist or print shop to assist you.

7

Getting Past the Gatekeeper

The roll of the gatekeeper is to prevent their superiors from being needlessly interrupted—especially by unwanted and unsolicited sales calls. They are trained and adept at handling salespeople, and have seen every gimmick or trick they use. Before a salesperson can sell to the decision maker, he or she must first sell the gatekeeper.

IMPLICATIONS — WHAT THIS MEANS TO YOU

One of the pitfalls salespeople stumble into when dealing with gatekeepers is developing a condescending attitude toward them. Most fail to realize their importance and responsibilities and the ultimate authority and influence they carry.

Gatekeepers have the ability to smooth the way for a salesperson or to immediately shut the door on them. As such, salespeople must not underestimate the power and influence the gatekeeper may have on a decision maker. Their position may be low on the organizational chart, but their power can be a vital force and influence. Salespeople must respect their abilities and influence if they wish to develop the rapport they need to get to the decision maker.

STRATEGIES, TIPS & TECHNIQUES TO APPLY

Salespeople will typically encounter two levels of gatekeepers. The initial gatekeeper at a company is the receptionist or switchboard operator. The second is the decision maker's assistant or executive secretary. It is important that salespeople not confuse the two because each requires a specific strategy for dealing with them effectively. Salespeople should be aware that there will be times when the decision maker's executive secretary or assistant may be filling in for the receptionist, so they must be careful about their attitudes and behaviors at all times.

Receptionists

Most receptionists are responsible for screening all calls to direct them to who he or she feels is the most appropriate individual, whether or not that person is the decision maker the salesperson is attempting to contact. If salespeople wish to avoid being grilled, screened, rejected or even disconnected, they must build rapport with the receptionist by being polite, to the point, and self-aware of the purpose behind their contact.

One of the most successful techniques is to ask to speak with the decision maker's executive secretary or assistant rather than directly to the decision maker. This resolves most of the problems salespeople encounter at this level. Before they make an initial call, they should call to verify the spelling of the decision maker's name as a pretense for the call, and additionally, ask the name of the decision maker's executive secretary or assistant. When they then make a cold call, they can ask for that individual by name. Many times, the call will be directly placed to that individual.

Executive Secretary or Assistant

Executive secretaries and assistants should be respected and handled as powerful allies. Salespeople should treat these individuals as if he or she is speaking for the decision maker. In most cases these individuals are privy to confidential information, and it is not wrong to assume they have the authority to speak for the decision maker. They hold a great deal of power and their authority should be openly recognized. In this regard, salespeople should use the exact same opening statement that they would use for the ultimate decision maker. They should pause and listen for objections and solicit feedback, reactions and advice. Salespeople who can make allies of the executive secretary or assistant will experience much easier access to the decision maker. These individuals are able to give the salesperson recommendations that will greatly assist them in getting the sale. They can also inform the salesperson of the best times and ways to contact the decision maker. These are exceptional resources that salespeople need to develop and foster if they wish to make the sale.

POINTS TO PONDER — SOMETHING TO THINK ABOUT

1. Have you been stymied by a gatekeeper in your attempts to reach a decision maker?
2. Do you personally distinguish between the receptionist and the executive secretary or assistant in your approach to either one?

TRAINING ACTIVITY — APPLICATION & ACTION PLAN

Put the techniques taught in this lesson into practice.

1. Identify a target company and determine who the decision maker is.
2. Call the company's main telephone number to verify the spelling of the name and ask the name of the decision maker's executive secretary or assistant.
3. Call back and ask to speak with the executive secretary or assistant.
4. Follow the steps detailed above and treat the executive secretary or assistant as the decision maker.
5. Start with your opening statement and solicit feedback.
6. Follow the executive secretary or assistant's advice and move the sale forward.

8

The First Thirty Seconds

The single biggest obstacle to any sale occurs in the initial 30 seconds of the first cold call. Prospects quickly categorize and pigeonhole a salesperson to determine whether their valuable time and work should be interrupted, and a poor initial perception may be extremely difficult to overcome.

IMPLICATIONS — WHAT THIS MEANS TO YOU

The first 30 seconds of a new business relationship is fraught with dangers and is the most precarious point of the sale. If the salesperson flounders or fails at this point, the entire sale can be lost and difficult to recover.

At the starting point, the prospect makes multiple judgments and decisions based purely on the initial perceptions created. Salespeople that are not careful about the perceptions they initially project, face more rejection and failure than salespeople who manage every aspect of their appearance, demeanor and attitude. Successful salespeople carefully manage the perceptions they create.

STRATEGIES, TIPS & TECHNIQUES TO APPLY

When salespeople initially approach a new prospect, a quick decision is made whether or not to allow the salesperson to proceed. In reality, the prospect is making countless judgments based upon the multiple perceptions a salesperson creates within 30 seconds or less.

The human mind is capable of receiving and processing thousands of inputs per second. This happens so rapidly most customers are unaware of the unconscious decisions they make. The judgment process determines the prospect's inward feelings of trustworthiness he or she has about the salesperson. The final decision moves the sales process forward, or stops the attempt because it is not worth their effort and time.

How the salesperson appears and presents him or herself is factored into these countless decisions. Before the salesperson says a single word, the prospect has already made a judgment on the salesperson's professional appearance. This includes physical appearance, personal hygiene, grooming and clothing. The next decisions are based upon the salesperson's posture, demeanor and attitude.

All prospects have expectations of how a salesperson should appear, especially if they represent a well-known company or organization. When these expectations are not met, an immediate judgment is made.

What is puzzling for many salespeople is that what works well for one company may completely fail at another. However, it is better for salespeople to err on the side of more conservative dress.

The initial judgments a customer makes about a salesperson's appearance and demeanor occur in a fraction of a second. Before a salesperson has an opportunity to say a word, major judgments have already been made. This either places prospects at ease or puts them in a defensive posture.

The next judgment can be made about the salesperson's handshake. Too strong or weak of a handshake creates a negative judgment. Salespeople should develop a firm handshake that reflects their competent nature.

After these initial nonverbal judgments, another is made on the salesperson's voice, tone, grammar, diction and enunciation. Poor grammar, diction and enunciation can rapidly undermine a salesperson's credibility. Despite expertise and experience, poor speaking habits project incompetence.

Finally, after a series of important decisions and judgments, the salesperson makes his or her initial presentation. In most instances, the prospect has already made the decision whether or not the salesperson has anything worthwhile to present.

Fortunately, a salesperson can quickly alter initial perceptions by using a strong opening to demonstrate to the prospect his or her product's value. A powerful opening includes an effectively delivered statement that elicits the prospect's interest.

Salespeople can carefully manage their initial perceptions to ensure they don't create needless barriers to the sale. This includes being neatly dressed and well groomed. If speaking skills are a problem, salespeople should gain outside assistance to help them overcome deficiencies. Often local teachers can tutor the salesperson until they are able to speak fluently and project their voice effectively.

POINTS TO PONDER — SOMETHING TO THINK ABOUT

1. How careful are you about the personal perceptions you create in the prospect's mind?
2. Have you ever seen potential sales quickly disappear without any obvious reason? Do you think they could have been influenced by any factors identified in this lesson?

TRAINING ACTIVITY — APPLICATION & ACTION PLAN

Conduct a personal assessment of your appearance by rating the following:

- Physical Appearance
- Grooming
- Clothing
- Posture
- Demeanor

- Attitude
- Enthusiasm
- Voice
- Tone
- Diction
- Enunciation
- Grammar

About the Author

Timothy F. Bednarz, Ph.D. is CEO of the American Management Development Group, Inc. For over 20 years he has researched, designed and authored hundreds of learning and development programs used by Fortune 1000 companies.

He is also the author of *Great! What Makes Leaders Great. What They Did, How They Did It and What You Can Learn from It* (2011).

Speaking Availability

Timothy F. Bednarz, Ph.D. is available for speaking engagements for your next meeting or association event. He can be contacted at 800-654-4935 or by e-mail at timothy.bednarz@majorium.com.

Bulk Sales

Bulk sales of this book or any other titles available from Majorium Business Press. Inquiries can be directed to sales@majorium.com, or by phone at 800-6654-4935.

Quick Order Form

Fax orders: 715-342-1118. Send this form.

Telephone orders: Call 800-654-4935 toll-free. Have your credit card ready.

Email orders: sales@majorium.com

Postal orders: Majorium Business Press, 2025 Main Street, Stevens Point, WI 54481, USA.

Please send the following books:

____

____

____

____

Please send more FREE information on:

❑Catalog ❑Speaking/Seminars ❑Mailing Lists ❑Consulting

Name: ________________________________

Address: ________________________________

City: __________________ State: _____ Zip: ________

Telephone: ________________________________

Email address: ____________________________

Sales tax: Please add 5.5% for products shipped to Wisconsin addresses.

Shipping by air:

United States: $4.00 for first book and $2.00 for each additional product.

International: $9.00 for first book; $5.00 for each additional product (estimate).

Made in the USA
Monee, IL
08 November 2026

67382833R00026